THIS
BOOK
BELONGS
TO

_____

Switching on the Moon

A Very First Book of
Bedtime Poems

collected by **Jane Yolen**
and **Andrew Fusek Peters**

illustrated by **G. Brian Karas**

CANDLEWICK PRESS

Contents

In Good Hands

Wherever night falls
The earth is always there
To catch it.

—*Roger McGough*

The Man in the Moon

The man in the moon
Looked out of the moon,
And this is what he said,
'Tis time that, now I'm getting up,
All babies went to bed.

—Mother Goose

Evening Shifts

As cloak-black clouds

Of evening drift

Across his torch-white eye,

The moon begins

His evening shift—

Nightwatchman of the sky.

—Graham Denton

Going
to
Bed

Tasty

How strange that someone thinks it nice

to eat the moon—a giant slice.

I wonder if he finds it kind

to leave a bit of rind behind.

—*Marilyn Singer*

From **The Moon's the North Wind's Cooky**
(What the Little Girl Said)

The Moon's the North Wind's cooky,

He bites it, day by day,

Until there's but a rim of scraps

That crumble all away.

—*Vachel Lindsay*

The Star

Twinkle, twinkle, little star,
How I wonder what you are!
Up above the world so high,
Like a diamond in the sky.

When the blazing sun is gone,
When he nothing shines upon,
Then you show your little light,
Twinkle, twinkle, all the night.

—*Jane Taylor*

The Starlighter

When the bat's on the wing and the bird's in the tree,
Comes the old Starlighter, whom none may see.

First in the West, where the low hills are,
He touches his wand to the Evening Star.

Then swiftly he runs on his rounds on high
Till he's lit every lamp in the dark blue sky.

—Arthur Guiterman

Go to Bed, Tom

Go to bed, Tom,
Go to bed, Tom,
Tired or not, Tom,
Go to bed, Tom.

—*Anonymous*

Going to Bed

Go to bed early—
Your hair grows curly.

Go to bed late—
Your hair grows straight.

Go to bed not at all—
Your hair will fall,
And you'll be bald
As a billiard ball.

—Colin West

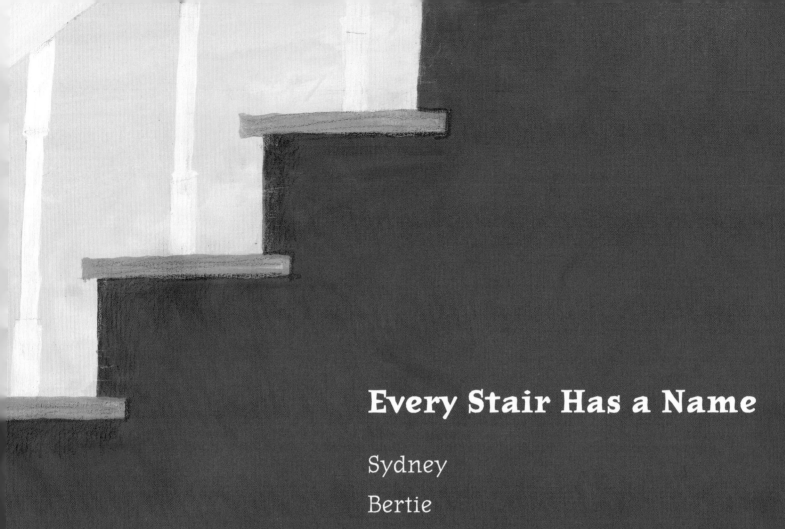

Every Stair Has a Name

Sydney

Bertie

Claribel

Sally

Ali

Ne'er-Do-Well

Creaky

Squeaky

Iggy

Fred

March straight on and into bed.

—Jill Townsend

Bathtime!

I've brushed my teeth,
I've scrubbed my knees
and I've really rubbed my neck!
I promise I've washed
behind my ears,
I promise I've done my back!

I've rubbed, I've scrubbed,
I've pummelled,
without a single groan!
I've brushed and splashed,
I've sploshed and splished . . .
I can manage ALL ALONE!

—*Judith Nicholls*

Naughty Soap Song

Just when I'm ready to
Start on my ears,
This is the time that my
Soap disappears.

It jumps from my fingers and
Slithers and slides
Down to the end of the
Tub, where it hides.

And acts in a most diso-
Bedient way
AND THAT'S WHY MY SOAP'S
GROWING THINNER EACH DAY.

—Dorothy Aldis

Bath Time Pirate

My name is Captain Soapsuds—
A mighty ship I sail.
I love to feel the sea mist
And hear the cold wind wail.

I count my bags of treasure.
I make men walk the plank.
I wish I had more fingers
To count the ships I sank.

When big sea serpents see me,
It merely makes me shrug.
I'm Captain Suds the pirate,
Till Mommy pulls the plug.

—Robert Scotellaro

Bath

Why can't I go to bed dirty?

What's so special about being clean?

I am dirty today. I'll get dirty again.

So why bother to wash in between?

—Jo Ellen Bogart

Bubble Song (for Bath Time)

If you blow
I will grow
to a trembling ball.

I'm a bubble of breath
in a shimmering shawl.

If you lift
I will drift
like a wisp of the air.

Then I'll burst with a gasp
and I'm simply not there.

—Tony Mitton

Bedtime Teeth

Scrub them, rub them
Sparkling white,
Swish them, whish them,
Grin goodnight.

—Lizann Flatt

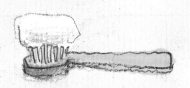

Which Brush?

I like a yellow brush,
Mum likes green,
Dad says his white brush
Gets teeth clean.
Ted's is red
And Sue's is blue,
And the baby doesn't care
Because her teeth aren't through.

—Kaye Umansky

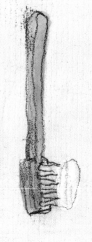

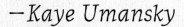
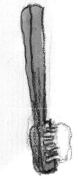

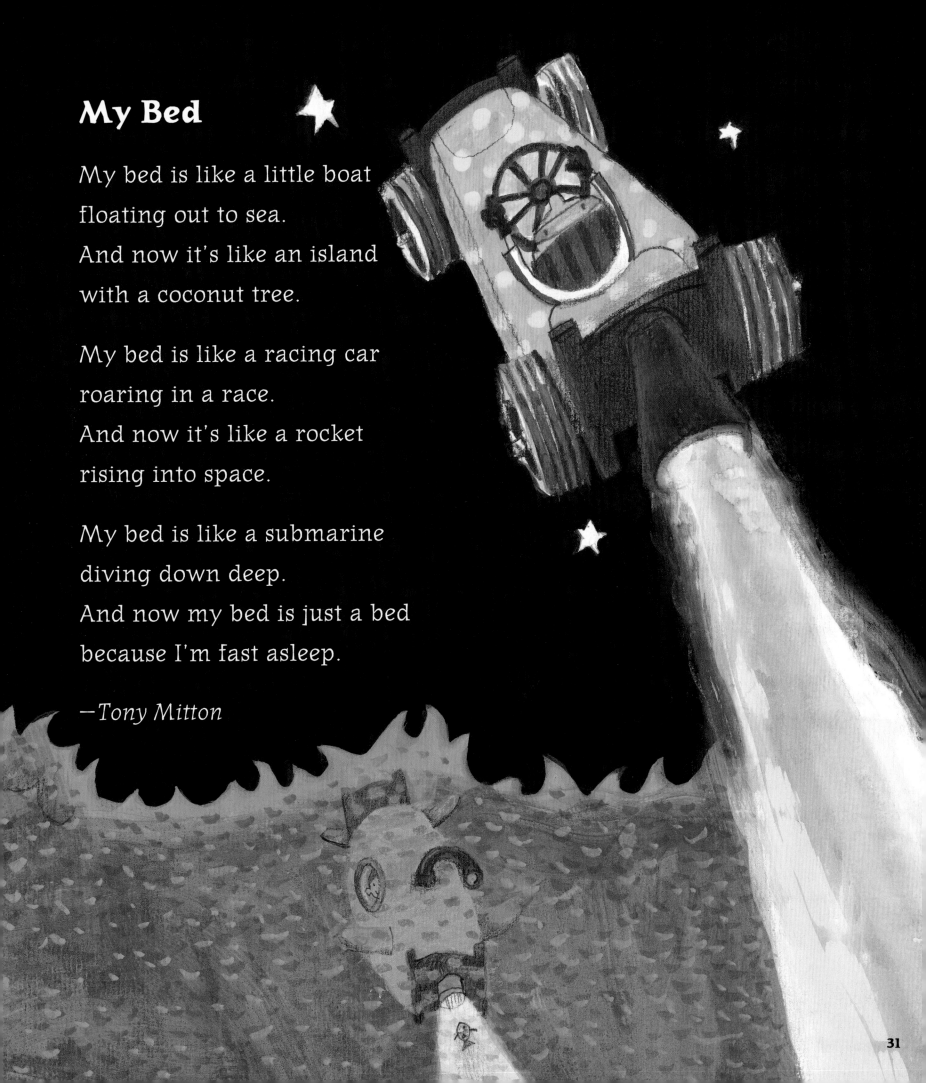

My Bed

My bed is like a little boat
floating out to sea.
And now it's like an island
with a coconut tree.

My bed is like a racing car
roaring in a race.
And now it's like a rocket
rising into space.

My bed is like a submarine
diving down deep.
And now my bed is just a bed
because I'm fast asleep.

—Tony Mitton

Snuggles

Work done

For the day

The sun

Switches on

The moon

Pulls

The clouds

Over its

Head and

Snuggles

Right down

Into the

Cosy bottom

Of the sky

—Roger McGough

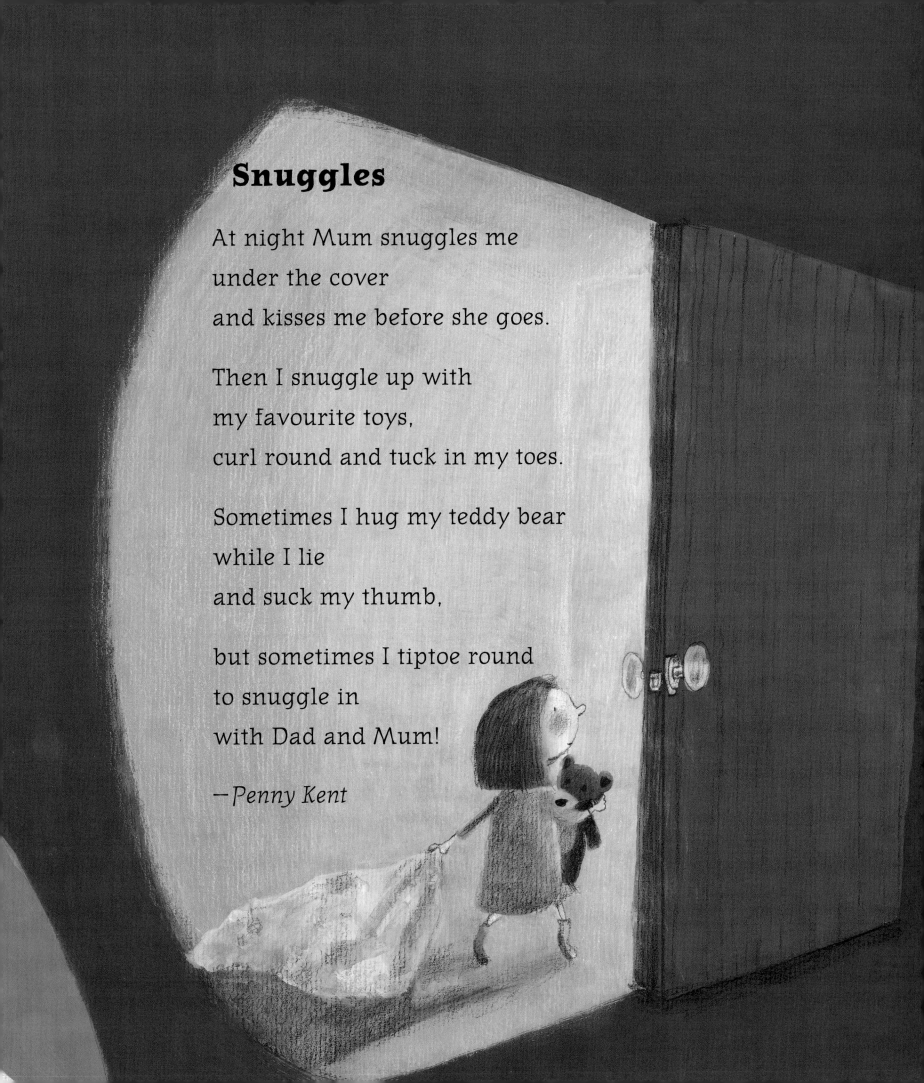

Snuggles

At night Mum snuggles me
under the cover
and kisses me before she goes.

Then I snuggle up with
my favourite toys,
curl round and tuck in my toes.

Sometimes I hug my teddy bear
while I lie
and suck my thumb,

but sometimes I tiptoe round
to snuggle in
with Dad and Mum!

—*Penny Kent*

Bedtime, Rhymetime

It's bedtime, it's rhymetime,
it's church bells cease their chimetime.

It's bedtime, it's teddytime,
it's pyjamas at the readytime.

It's bedtime, it's tunetime,
it's watch the milky moontime.

It's bedtime, it's blisstime,
it's one more goodnight kisstime.

—John Rice

From *The Bed Book*

O who cares much
if a Bed's big or small
or lumpy and bumpy—
who cares at all
as long as its springs
are bouncy and new.

From a Bounceable Bed
you bounce into the blue—
over the hollyhocks
(Toodle-oo!)
over the owls'
to-whit-to-whoo,
over the moon
to Timbuktoo
with springier springs
than a kangaroo.

—*Sylvia Plath*

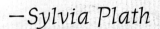

Little Bear Sleeping

Moon peeks over a distant hill.
Wind comes rattling as the old wind will.
"Hush," says the moon, "be still, be still—
there's a little bear sleeping on the windowsill."

—Alice Schertle

Teddy Bear, Teddy Bear

Teddy Bear, Teddy Bear,
Go upstairs.
Teddy Bear, Teddy Bear,
Say your prayers.
Teddy Bear, Teddy Bear,
Turn out the light.
Teddy Bear, Teddy Bear,
Say good night.

—*Anonymous*

Goodnight Mummy

Goodnight Mummy
Goodnight Roo
Goodnight Tigger
Goodnight Pooh

Goodnight Mummy
Goodnight Cat
Goodnight Squeaker
(My pet rat)

Goodnight Billy
Goodnight Sis
Goodnight cousins
and Auntie Liz

Goodnight Mummy
And all living creatures
Goodnight elephants
Goodnight teachers

Goodnight moths
Goodnight bees
Goodnight ankles
Goodnight knees

Goodnight spiders
Goodnight ants
Goodnight trousers
Goodnight pants

Goodnight Mummy
Goodnight sun
Goodnight every . . .
everyone

—*Roger Stevens*

Nighttime

How do dreams know
    when to creep

Into my head
    as I fall off
    to sleep?

—*Lee Bennett Hopkins*

Sweet
Dreams

Mama Bird's Lullaby

Come fluttering
into your nest.
Night is here,
it's time to rest.

Tuck your head
beneath a wing.
Quiet now.
Let mama sing,

a song to you
of twig and sky.
A tender napping
lullaby,

while you dream
of seed and lawn,
my little bird
of chirp and yawn,

my sleepy bird
so wild and blue,
I sing this lullaby
to you.

—*Rebecca Kai Dotlich*

The Mouse's Lullaby

Oh, rock-a-by, baby mouse, rock-a-by, so!
When baby's asleep to the baker's I'll go,
And while he's not looking I'll pop from a hole,
And bring to my baby a fresh penny roll.

—Palmer Cox

Switch

Tonight my puppy woke me up
by climbing in my bed.
His cushion looks so comfortable
I'll sleep on it instead.
If he dreams of ice cream cones
and trips to outer space,
will I dream of chewy bones
and finding cats to chase?

—*Marilyn Singer*

Mermaid's Lullaby

Hush, foam mocker,
Sleep, wave maker,
Close your eyes and dream,
Tide breaker.

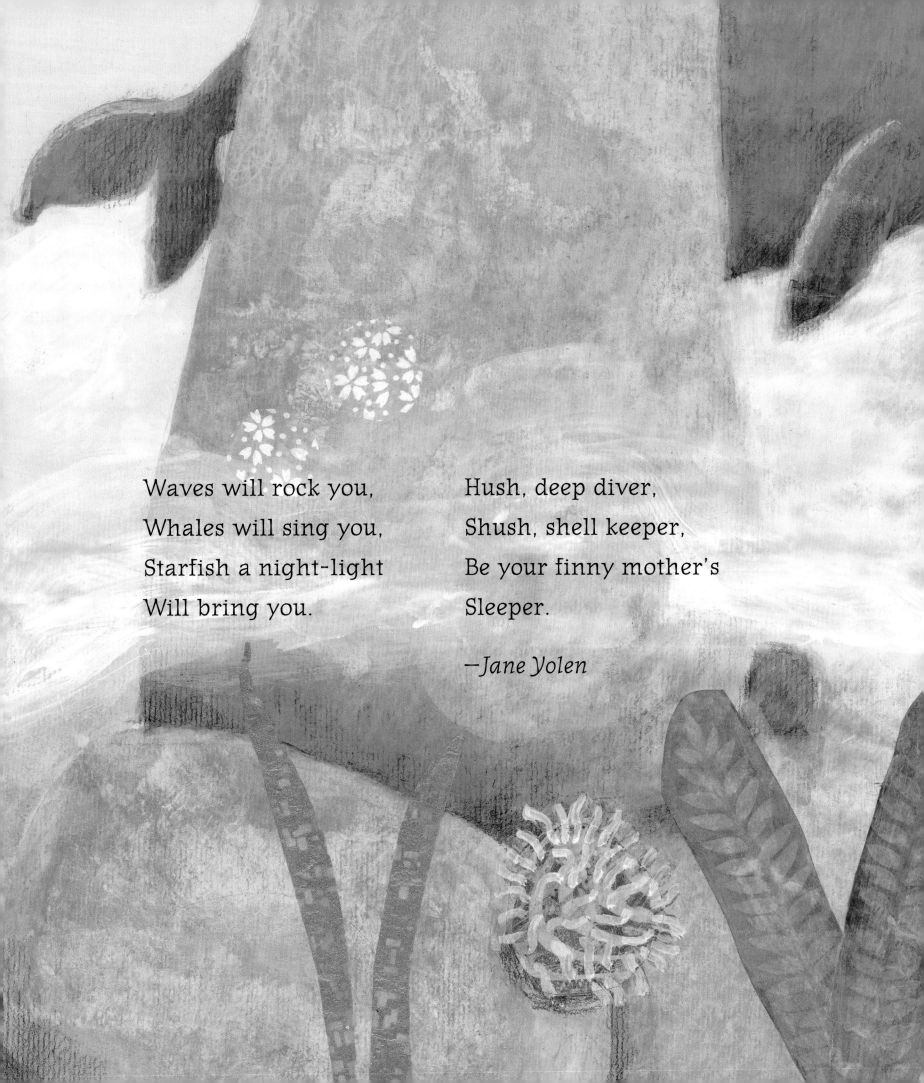

Waves will rock you,
Whales will sing you,
Starfish a night-light
Will bring you.

Hush, deep diver,
Shush, shell keeper,
Be your finny mother's
Sleeper.

—Jane Yolen

Sweet and Low

Sweet and low, sweet and low,

Wind of the western sea,

Low, low, breathe and blow,

Wind of the western sea!

Over the rolling waters go,

Come from the dying moon, and blow,

Blow him again to me;

While my little one, while my pretty one, sleeps.

Sleep and rest, sleep and rest,

Father will come to thee soon;

Rest, rest, on mother's breast,

Father will come to thee soon;

Father will come to his babe in the nest,

Silver sails all out of the west

Under the silver moon;

Sleep, my little one, sleep, my pretty one, sleep.

—Alfred, Lord Tennyson

Night Noises in the City

In the country
Things are quiet.
In the city
Noise runs riot.

Car horns beep.
Buses boom.
People shout.
Trucks zoom-zoom.

Fire engine
Siren wails,
Someone whistles
Taxi hails.

Garbage truck
Churns crackety-crack.
Subway rails
Go clickety-clack.

Close your eyes
And use your ears.
And hear what
A city sleeper hears.

—Jane Yolen

Lullaby of the Iroquois

Little brown baby-bird, lapped in your nest,
　　Wrapped in your nest,
　　Strapped in your nest,
Your straight little cradle-board rocks you to rest;
　　Its hands are your nest;
　　Its bands are your nest;
It swings from the down-bending branch of the oak;
You watch the camp flame, and the curling gray smoke;
But, oh, for your pretty black eyes sleep is best,—
Little brown baby of mine, go to rest.

Little brown baby-bird swinging to sleep,
    Winging to sleep,
    Singing to sleep,
Your wonder-black eyes that so wide open keep,
    Shielding their sleep,
    Unyielding to sleep,
The heron is homing, the plover is still,
The night-owl calls from his haunt on the hill,
Afar the fox barks, afar the stars peep,—
Little brown baby of mine, go to sleep.

—E. Pauline Johnson (Tekahionwake)

From **Dream Angus**

Dreams to sell, fine dreams to sell,

Angus is coming with dreams to sell.

Hush now wee bairnie and sleep without fear,

For Angus will bring you a dream, my dear.

—George Churchill

The Dream Keeper

Bring me all of your dreams,

You dreamers,

Bring me all of your

Heart melodies

That I may wrap them

In a blue cloud-cloth

Away from the too-rough fingers

Of the world.

—*Langston Hughes*

From *The Cozy Book*

And now the cozy day is gone
And now the cozy book is read
Of all the cozy things there are
The coziest of all is bed
So go to sleep, sweet sleepyhead
Just curl up snug and shut the light
A goodnight hug, a kiss goodnight

Sweet thoughts
Sweet dreams
Sleep deep
Sleep tight

Droopy
Drifty
Drowsy
Dozy
Dream of everything that's cozy

—*Mary Ann Hoberman*

Rock-a-bye, Baby

Rock-a-bye, baby,
On the treetop.
When the wind blows,
The cradle will rock.
When the bough breaks,
The cradle will fall,
And down will come baby,
Cradle and all.

—*Traditional lullaby*

Rack-a-bye, Baby

Rack-a-bye, baby,

Pon tap a tree tap,

Wen de win blow

De crib a go swing;

Wen de lim bruck

De crib a go drap,

Den lim, crib, an baby,

Eberyting drap. BRAP!

—*Traditional West Indian lullaby*

Rockabye Tent Peg

The wind has fingers. *Knock! Knock! Knock!*
My tent's a cradle, watch it rock.

The ground is bumpy where I lie
My sister gives a snuffly sigh

The campfire glows like a sleepy star
The river sings from near to far

With a zip, I'm wrapped up tight
    As the moon goes camping in the
    night

        —Andrew Fusek Peters

Night Song

When the sun has set
And night has come,
The insect chorus
Starts to hum.

And nothing else
Is there to hear,
But the insect voices
Soft and clear.

The insects hum
In sweet delight,
Singing their praises
Of the night.

—*Leland B. Jacobs*

Sleeping Outdoors

Under the dark is a star,
Under the star is a tree,
Under the tree is a blanket,
And under the blanket is me.

—*Marchette Chute*

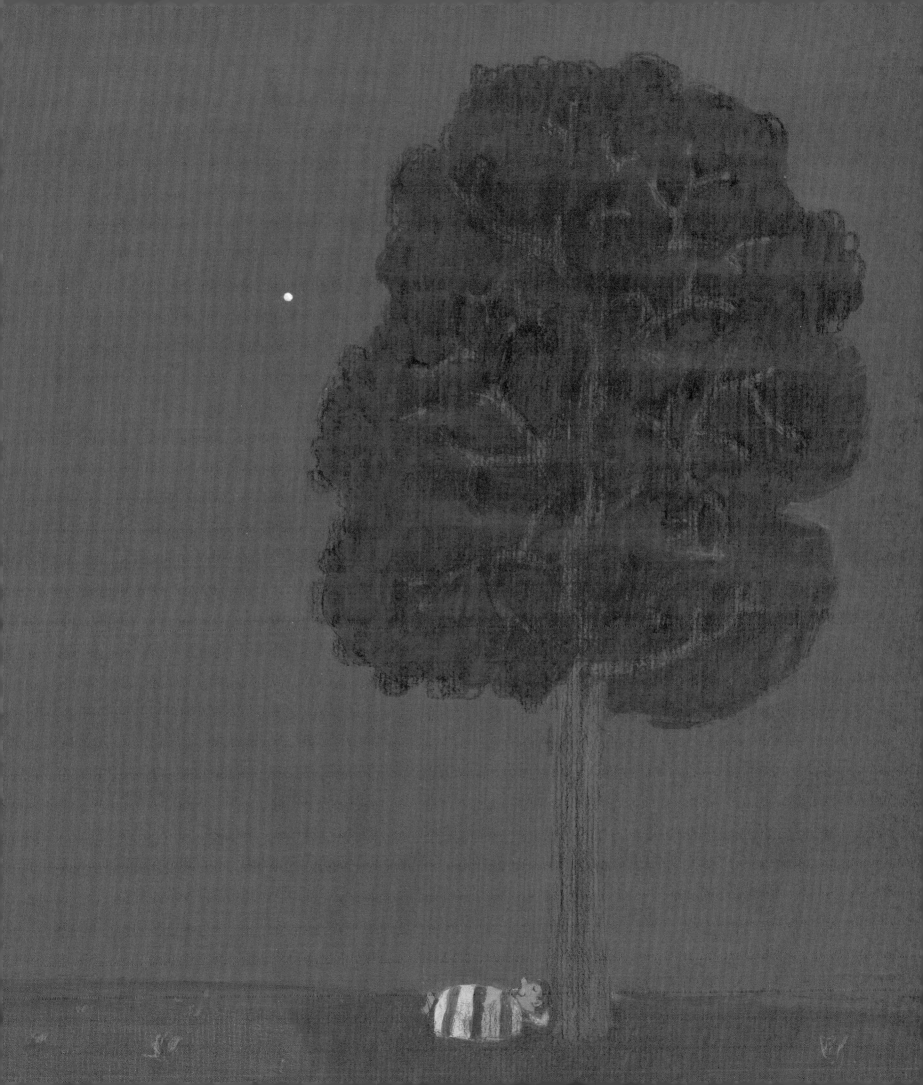

Twinkle Twinkle Firefly

Twinkle

Twinkle

Firefly

In the dark

It's you I spy

Over the river

Over the bush

Twinkle

Twinkle

Firefly

For the traveller

passing by

Over the river

Over the bush

Twinkle

Twinkle

Firefly

Lend the dark

your sparkling eye

—John Agard

Wordless Words

Wordless words.

A tuneless tune.

Blow out the sun.

Draw down the shade.

Turn off the dog.

Snap on the stars.

Unwrap the moon.

Wish leafy, sleeping trees good night

And listen

To the day shut tight.

—Karla Kuskin

Bedtime Chant for the Tooth Fairy

Oak, ash, weeping willow,
Lay your tooth beneath the pillow.

Rock, pebble, grain of sand,
Set your sail for sleepy land.

Ember, flame, fire-bright,
Fairy footsteps in the night.

Robin redbreast, swallow, swift,
Wake to find a silver gift.

—*Polly Peters*

A Flash

Through the night
A streak of light,
Meteorite.

—*Rick Walton*

In
the
Night

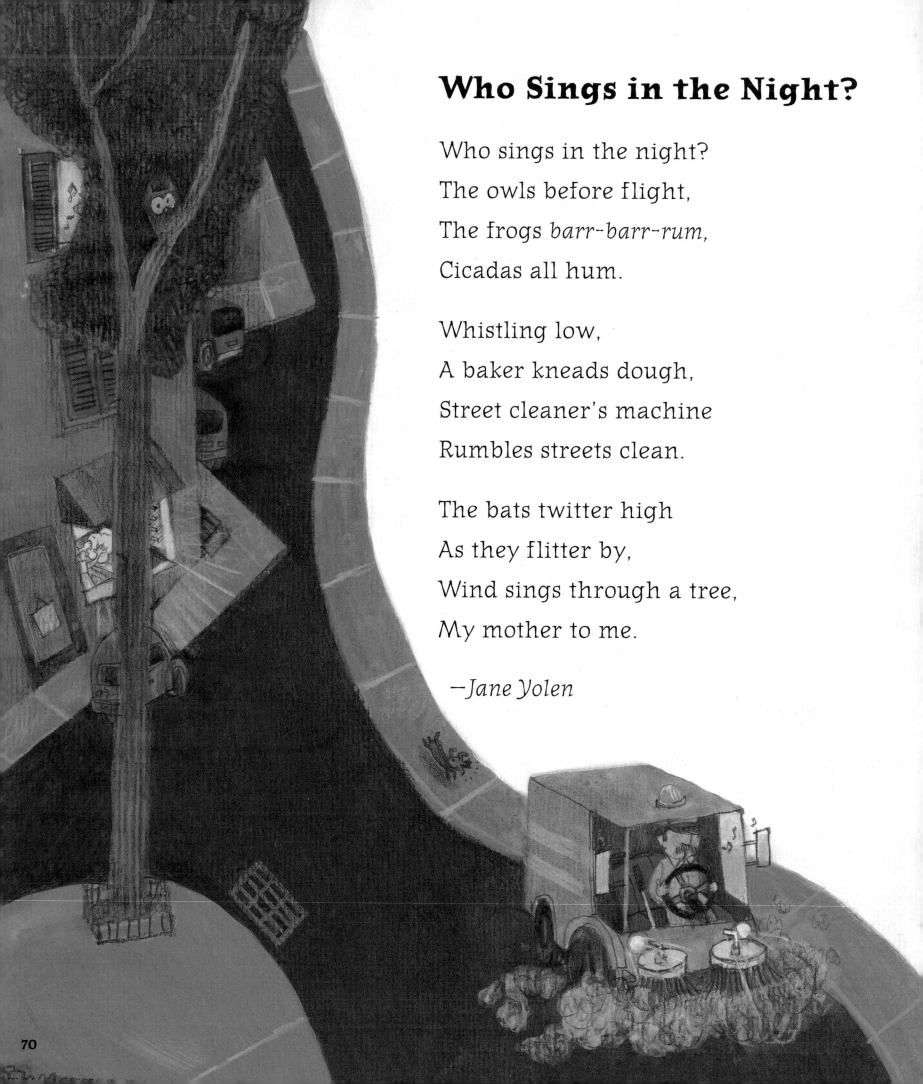

Who Sings in the Night?

Who sings in the night?
The owls before flight,
The frogs *barr-barr-rum,*
Cicadas all hum.

Whistling low,
A baker kneads dough,
Street cleaner's machine
Rumbles streets clean.

The bats twitter high
As they flitter by,
Wind sings through a tree,
My mother to me.

—Jane Yolen

Night Sounds

The hoot of an owl
The creak of the stair
The swing of the door
The whisper of air

The rustle of clothes
The patter of feet
The shiver of breath
The huff of the sheet

There's somebody here
You take a quick peep
The kiss of a kiss
Hush. Go to sleep.

—Roger Stevens

Here You Lie

Here you lie
Warm in bed
Feather pillow
For your head.

In the dark
Town fox prowls,
Brown owl swoops,
Guard dog growls.

In the dark
Cold winds blow,
Tom cat creeps,
White stars glow.

Here you lie
Warm in bed
Feather pillow
For your head.

—Wes Magee

In the Night

When I wake up and it is dark
    And very far from day
I sing a humming sort of tune
    To pass the time away.

I hum it loud, I hum it soft,
    I hum it low and deep,
And by the time I'm out of breath
    I've hummed myself to sleep.

—*Marchette Chute*

Little Shadows
(Or why there's no need to fear the dark)

In the absence of light
Little shadows, in fright,
Cling tightly together
And call themselves Night.

—*Philip Waddell*

The Bat

The bat is batty as can be.

It sleeps all day in cave or tree,

And when the sun sets in the sky,

It rises from its rest to fly.

All night this mobile mammal mugs

A myriad of flying bugs.

And after its night out on the town,

The batty bat sleeps

Upside down.

—Douglas Florian

Stars with Wings

Sometimes it seems
like all the stars
have fallen
from the skies,
but when I see
the stars have wings
I know they're fireflies.

—Betsy Franco

Wonder

I wonder at the stars by night

These little chandeliers of light

I wonder if in turn they see

The tiny spark that makes up me?

—Andrew Fusek Peters

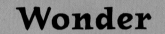

Night Light

Twinkle, twinkle, little star,
I know what you really are:
a blinking bug in flickering flight,
lighting up my yard tonight,
in the treetops, near the ground,
winking, flashing all around.
I watch you and I'm mystified—
how did you get that bulb inside?

—*Cynthia Cotten*

Shepherd's Night Count

One ewe,

One ram,

Two sheep,   One lock,

One lamb,   Five folds,

Three sheep,   One light,

One flock,   Good dog,

Four gates,   Good night.

—*Jane Yolen*

Puff

Lying, half awake, in bed,
Close those eyes and rest your head.

Cannot, will not, shall not, can't
Give in to sleep—so here's a chant.

See a candle, burning bright.
See the circle of its light.

In that circle, you and me,
Those we love and family.

All together, join and say,
"Bad dreams! Puff! All blown away!"

May the circle of the light
Bring the brightest dreams tonight.

All is safe. Now drift away
On velvet dreams, from night to day.

—Polly Peters

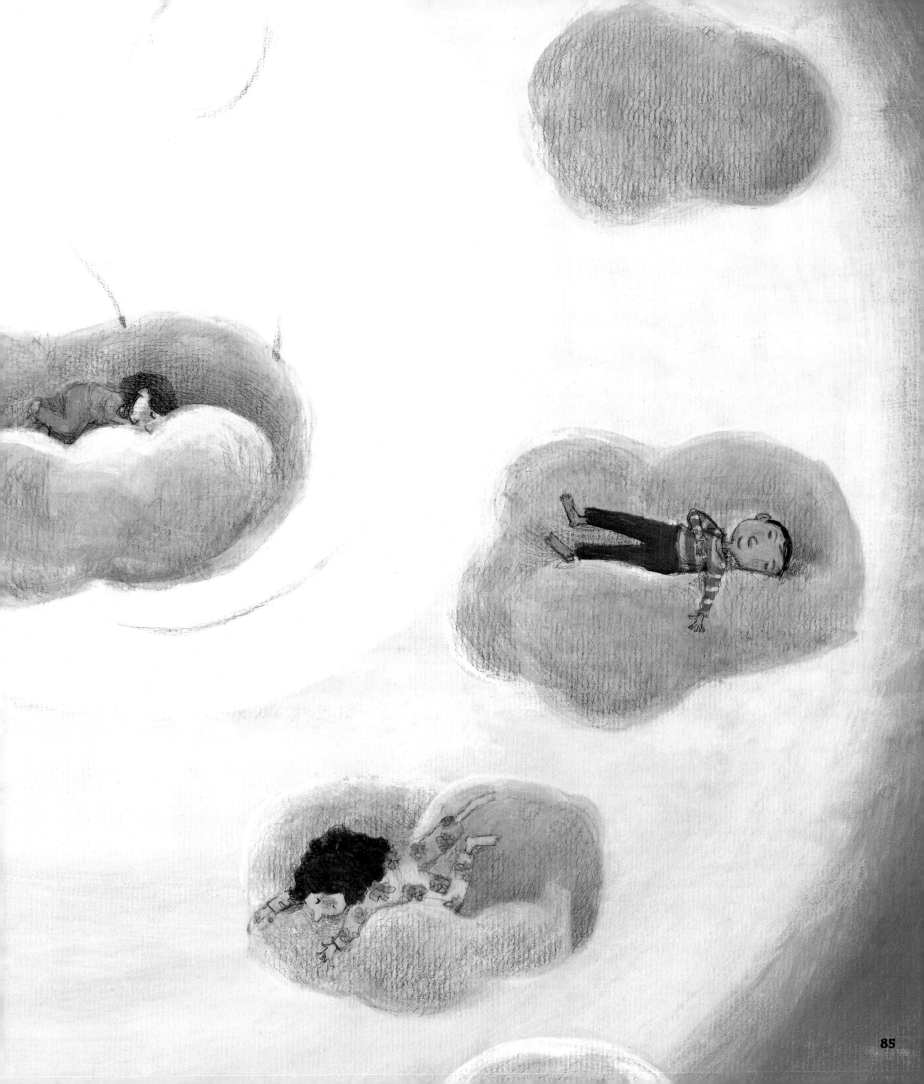

Rain Song

Rockabye raindrops
Fall from the sky;
They tapdance on tiles
A wild lullaby.

They gush through the gutters.
On smooth windowpanes,
They scribble and scrabble,
Then gargle down drains

To spatter and scatter
In silvery streams
With a cradle of wind
And rockabye dreams.

—*Andrew Fusek Peters*

Night Sounds

When I lie in bed

I think I can hear

The stars being switched on

I think I can

And I think I can hear

The moon

Breathing

But I have to be still

So still.

All the house is sleeping.

Except for me.

Then I think I can hear it.

—Berlie Doherty

The Night Will Never Stay

The night will never stay,
The night will still go by,
Though with a million stars
You pin it to the sky;
Though you bind it with the blowing wind
And buckle it with the moon,
The night will slip away
Like sorrow or a tune.

—*Eleanor Farjeon*

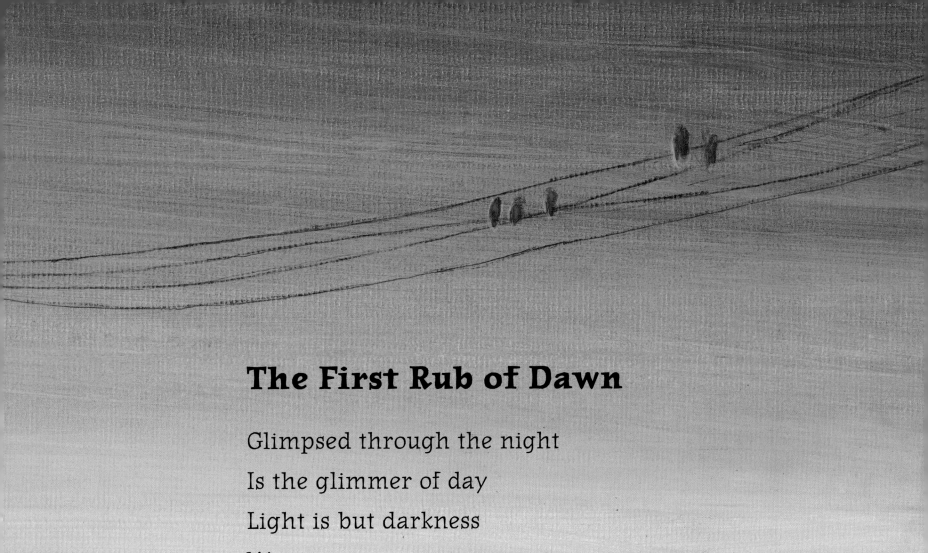

The First Rub of Dawn

Glimpsed through the night

Is the glimmer of day

Light is but darkness

Worn away

—*Roger McGough*

☆ Index of First Lines ☆

☆ Index of Poets ☆

☆ Copyright Acknowledgments ☆

For Olivia and Christian, sweet dreams!

G. B. K.

For all the Stemple poetry lovers,
Who love to read between the covers,
And for the other poets—the Piatts—
For whom good poems make quiet riots

J. Y.

This one is to Jai, only little now
but growing every day (and night)

A. F. P.

Compilation copyright © 2010 by Jane Yolen and Andrew Fusek Peters
Illustrations copyright © 2010 by G. Brian Karas
Copyright acknowledgments appear on pages 94–95.

This collection gathers poems from various parts of the English-speaking world,
including Great Britain, the Caribbean, Australia, and the United States. Regional
spellings and usage have been retained in order to preserve the integrity of the originals.

First edition 2010

Library of Congress Cataloging-in-Publication Data

Switching on the moon : a very first book of bedtime poems / collected by
Jane Yolen and Andrew Fusek Peters ; illustrated by G. Brian Karas. —1st ed.
p. cm.
Includes index.
ISBN 978-0-7636-4249-5
1. Night—Juvenile poetry. 2. Sleep—Juvenile poetry. 3. Bedtime—Juvenile poetry.
4. Children's poetry, American. 5. Children's poetry, English. 6. Lullabies, English—United States.
7. Lullabies, English. I. Yolen, Jane. II. Peters, Andrew (Andrew Fusek) III. Karas, G. Brian, ill. IV. Title.

PS595.N54S95 2010
398.8—dc22   2008025442

10 11 12 13 14 15 16 SCP 10 9 8 7 6 5 4 3 2 1

Printed in Humen, Dongguan, China

This book was typeset in Journal.
The illustrations were done in gouache, acrylic, and pencil.

Candlewick Press
99 Dover Street
Somerville, Massachusetts 02144

visit us at www.candlewick.com